TUESDA

MW01609135

By

DANIEL ARNOLD and MEDINA HAHN

Dramatic Publishing
Woodstock, Illinois • England • Australia • New Zealand

*** NOTICE ***

This play is dedicated to the memory of Mary and William.

IMPORTANT BILLING AND CREDIT REQUIREMENTS

TUESDAYS & SUNDAYS was originally produced at Theatre Network's NeXtFest in June 2000, with the following cast and crew:

WILLIAM . . . . Daniel Arnold
MARY . . . . Medina Hahn

Director / Dramaturg . . . . Wojtek Kozlinski
Designer. . . . . Catherine Mudryk
Stage Manager . . . . Andrew Brooks

AUTHORS' NOTES:

Leading up to the year 2000 there was a significant escalation of youth violence and school shootings around the world. During that time, we came across this true story of two young lovers from the 1800s and it broke our hearts. We realized that these kinds of crimes had always been happening, that people had always been hurting each other—out of pain or fear. We wrote this play as an attempt to understand why. Why is it that fear takes over so often? Why doesn't love always prevail?

Tuesdays & Sundays is inspired by true events. It is by no means the true story—for the absolute truth will never be known.

A NOTE ON STYLE:

The original production of *Tuesdays & Sundays* was performed by the authors. The set consisted of a small platform with a backdrop and some stepping stones on which most of the action was played. There were also a number of lanterns hanging about the stage which remained lit throughout the show. The effect was that of an outdoor setting, a riverbed, rocks, perhaps a bridge, and a starlit sky.

As William and Mary, we awoke into a void and started to remember and relive the story that brought us there—at a generally fast, and sometimes breakneck pace. There was no direct address to the audience, but there was an element of storytelling in that we would switch quickly and easily between two states of reality: "recalling" what was happening, as if seeing it before us for the very first time, thus allowing the audience to hear our thoughts, and then "playing the scene" with the other character. The shifts were achieved through simple changes of focus, a movement of the head or a difference in tone. Where the script indicates a kiss or holding hands, such actions were never physicalized, but only implied. Supporting characters were given distinct voices but not full characterizations.

As a guide, lines that begin without capitals and have limited punctuation indicate our state of "recalling." Lines that appear as proper sentences, starting with capitals and ending with punctuation, indicate "playing the scene."

That said, we have seen a production of *Tuesdays & Sundays* that used four actors—two sets of William and Mary: "the memories" who live the story, and "the spirits" who recall it. Lines were sometimes shared and sometimes said alone. This production used more physicality, often realistically acting out scenes, and the story still held together.

Therefore, the style of the script is a blank canvas; stage directions and beat indications are kept to a bare minimum, thus allowing room for imagination.

Daniel Arnold and Medina Hahn

ACKNOWLEDGMENTS:

Wojtek Kozlinski (this play would not be what it is without you), Catherine Mudryk, Theatre Network and the NeXtFest team, Charlie Tomlinson, Kim McKaw, Workshop West Theatre, Francis and Gretta Sitwell, Twilla MacLeod, Beth Graham, Daniela Vlaskalic, Adibi and Larry Hahn, Byran Everett Place, Shenta and Gary Arnold, Antje Oegel and Bret Adams Ltd., Edmonton Arts Council, Canada Council for the Arts and Alberta Foundation for the Arts.

TUESDAYS & SUNDAYS

A Play in One Act
For 1m., 1w., or 2m., 2w*

CHARACTERS:

WILLIAM. . . . . a farm boy, eighteen

MARY . . . . a farm girl, sixteen

SETTING: A memory of Margate, 1887.

APPROXIMATE RUNNING TIME: 50 minutes.

*See Authors' Notes (and a Note on Style) on pages 5 and 6.

TUESDAYS & SUNDAYS

(A sky of glowing lanterns. WILLIAM and MARY are discovered sitting, their eyes closed. Slowly, they begin to awake.)

WILLIAM   Where are we?

MARY   Heaven?

WILLIAM   Where are we?

MARY   Hell?

WILLIAM   Where are we?

BOTH   …Earth.

WILLIAM   Margate.

MARY   A rural community called

BOTH   Margate.

MARY   It's gorgeous. Beautiful winding roads

WILLIAM   can't go straight

9

MARY   tranquil flowing rivers

WILLIAM   field after field of potatoes

MARY   a rural community

WILLIAM   like any other rural community

MARY   none like this one

WILLIAM   peaceful

MARY   Heaven

(Beat.)

MARY   a Tuesday

WILLIAM   …yes, a Tuesday

MARY   that's where

WILLIAM   New Year's Eve

MARY   going to the Bryenton's

WILLIAM   yes

MARY   New Year's Eve

WILLIAM   going to the Bryenton's

MARY   yes

BOTH   A TUESDAY!

WILLIAM   farm boys scrub the rich red dirt from their
bodies

MARY   daughters of the farmers don their very best
frocks

WILLIAM   slick down their hair

MARY   fresh-faced

WILLIAM   bundle up

MARY   for the cold

WILLIAM   say good night to their parents with a promise
to behave

MARY   and leave in time to arrive before the sun
goes down...

WILLIAM   my friend Francis at the gate, with a bottle of
rum

MARY   with my older brother Jacob, we walk up
Mud Road

WILLIAM   sipping on the way

MARY   nervous and giddy

BOTH   the sun setting

WILLIAM   and the moon, Francis, look!

BOTH   the sun and the moon!

MARY   we walk by the light of the sun and the
              moon...

BOTH   A NEW YEAR'S EVE DANCE AT MR.
              AND MRS. BRYENTON'S!

WILLIAM   admission 25 cents

MARY   parents and grandparents, widows and pets

WILLIAM   admission 25 cents?

MARY   bachelors and maids and infants and lovers

BOTH   EVERYONE WELCOME

MARY   fiddling, punch, piano, a family affair

WILLIAM   little girls dance on their father's feet

MARY   little boys run from their mother's grasp

WILLIAM   the older girls, whispers in the corner

MARY   the older boys, stealing drinks out back

BOTH   we meet

WILLIAM   with a glance

MARY   by chance

WILLIAM   by the punch

BOTH   we meet

   (Beat.)

WILLIAM   You're a Tuplin, right?

MARY   That's right, how'd you know?

WILLIAM   I saw you come in with your brother.

MARY   You know my brother?

WILLIAM   Yes.

MARY   he gets me some punch

WILLIAM   I get her some punch

MARY   he spills on my hand

WILLIAM   I do?

MARY   yes you do but don't notice so neither do I

BOTH   we stand there

(Beat.)

MARY   I've seen you before, what's your name?

WILLIAM   Of course, how do you do, I'm—William Millman.

MARY   Mary Tuplin.

WILLIAM   Pleased to make your acquaintance.

MARY   "William meet Mary. Mary meet William."

WILLIAM   Thank you, Mr. Bryenton, we just met, sir, thank you. "She's soon to be seventeen, William, she's growing up quick!"

MARY   Thank you, Mrs. Bryenton, he knows we just met.

BOTH   "Well, well, carry on. This party's a success!"

WILLIAM   "my dear"

MARY   "mutter mutter"

WILLIAM   "my dear"

MARY   "mutter mutter"

BOTH   alone

(Beat.)

MARY   William Millman.

WILLIAM   Mary Tuplin...feet beneath the table

MARY   soft words in the corner

WILLIAM   I make her laugh

MARY   look at those couples, dancing so close

WILLIAM   I give her a drink

MARY   a smile

WILLIAM   a hand through the hair

MARY   getting to know you, sweet, exciting, soft,
              intriguing, getting to know

WILLIAM   trying to get

MARY   getting to know

WILLIAM   trying to get

BOTH   Flirting.

WILLIAM   Francis, my friend, just stands in the doorway

MARY   Francis, his friend

BOTH   just stands in the doorway

WILLIAM   and stares at the girl playing fiddle

MARY   my older brother Jacob

BOTH   finds a girl of his own

WILLIAM   Jacob, her brother

BOTH   is not a good chaperone!…

MARY   Just before midnight!

WILLIAM   all of us standing

MARY   music stopped, lights low

WILLIAM   Mrs. Bryenton standing on a chair

MARY   Mr. Bryenton beside, holding up his watch

WILLIAM   just before midnight!

BOTH   ten…nine…eight…

MARY   William takes my hand in his

BOTH   seven...six...five

MARY   I look at him, looking at me, we smile, we
              count

BOTH   four...three...two

MARY   no one's looking

BOTH   one

MARY   he kisses me

WILLIAM   Happy New Year...

(Beat.)

MARY   He Kisses Me...

WILLIAM   Happy New Year.

(Beat.)

MARY   We dance!

WILLIAM   she dances, I try

MARY   we dance, till forever, we dance till forever
              and a day with my head on his shoulder, his
              hands on my back till forever

WILLIAM   till four

MARY   till forever and

BOTH   our eyes closed

MARY   we kiss, till forever, my tiptoes, his hands, we kiss till forever and a day till forever

WILLIAM   till four...and then I walk her home!

MARY   he walks me home! I am sixteen going on seventeen.

WILLIAM   I am eighteen going on nineteen.

MARY   he's handsome

WILLIAM   she's...giddy!

MARY   he's...handsome!

WILLIAM   she's...!

MARY   William Millman.

WILLIAM   Mary Tuplin.

MARY   You're walking me home.

WILLIAM   So I am.

MARY   How many girls have you walked home in all your eighteen going on nineteen years?

WILLIAM   I've walked home my share of girls.

MARY   Have you really?

WILLIAM   No.

  (Beat.)

BOTH   A WALK HOME AT FOUR IN THE
           MORNING

WILLIAM   snow beneath our boots

MARY   my arm within his

WILLIAM   our breath in the air

MARY   the moon guiding us along Mud Road

WILLIAM   Did you see, earlier?

MARY   On the walk here?

WILLIAM   The sunset?

MARY   And the moon? I saw!

WILLIAM   Me too!

MARY   I saw!

WILLIAM   "Yes, I saw t-t-too!"

MARY   yells Francis from behind, following behind

WILLIAM   I can't believe I spend time with him!

MARY   Francis hears him and hollers

WILLIAM   "I heard th-that!"— Go home!

MARY   William yells and I tell him— Be nice.

WILLIAM   He told my folks he'd look after me so that's
            what he's doing.

MARY   Need looking after, do you?

WILLIAM   According to my folks— Go home!

MARY   he yells again with the bark of a man not a
            child not a youth but a man

WILLIAM   Just go.

MARY   Francis yells back

WILLIAM   "Mama's b-b-boy!"

(Beat.)

WILLIAM   on the bridge to cross the river...

BOTH   that bridge

MARY   to cross the river...

WILLIAM   we kick snow from the deck...

BOTH   watch it fall to the water below

MARY   and keep on

WILLIAM   before Francis catches up...

MARY   we talk

WILLIAM   and we tease

MARY   about respectability and properness

WILLIAM   at four in the morning with rum punch on our
              breath...we talk seriously awhile

MARY   about the meaning of life

WILLIAM   So who are you, Mary?

MARY   Just a girl, I think.

WILLIAM   Don't think too much or you won't be...just a
              girl...

        (Beat.)

MARY   he confuses me

WILLIAM   ...we don't talk at all

(Beat.)

MARY   he talks of his passion

WILLIAM   I play piano at service!

MARY   Oh, that's where I've seen you!

WILLIAM   Mr. Bryenton teaches me, and I'm getting
           quite good! I don't play every Sunday but
           pretty soon I will.

MARY   Yes, I knew I'd seen you before, yes, you
           play quite well. I remember, you play quite
           well indeed.

WILLIAM   Thank you, Mary Tuplin.

MARY   You're welcome, William Millman.

WILLIAM   I find this quite funny so I laugh and she—

MARY   Your laugh is funny.

WILLIAM   —she makes fun of my laugh

MARY   Your laugh is funny.

WILLIAM   Come now, Mary, don't tease.

MARY   I'm not teasing, William, I'm telling the truth.

WILLIAM   The truth? And you call yourself a
            respectable girl.

MARY   I am.

WILLIAM   Don't you know the "respectable" never tell
            the truth?

MARY   Yes they do.

WILLIAM   No, it's what makes them respectable, "Never
            tell the truth."

MARY   You know nothing.

WILLIAM   My my, we've grown up on different sides of
            the river, that's for sure.

MARY   That's for sure indeed. You talk nonsense.

WILLIAM   I may be a little drunk.

MARY   …and I give him a smile

WILLIAM   and I try to wink but it's four in the morning
            and I'm quite tired so both eyes go

BOTH   blink

WILLIAM   instead of a wink

BOTH   ...and we smile...

MARY   ...simply walk in silence now, down Mud
                Road, arm in arm

WILLIAM   past the Black Horse Inn

MARY   all of its lights out

WILLIAM   How is it that we've never met before?

MARY   I'm nearly three years younger than you.

WILLIAM   That's no reason, I've known girls way
                younger than you...

MARY   I've no wish to know what you mean by that.

   (Beat.)

WILLIAM   This your gate?

MARY   Yes it is...we walk up the lane

WILLIAM   I tell Francis to wait, he sits down at the gate
                and pulls out a pipe, "good l-l-luck" he says
                and I tell him—shut up

MARY   we walk up the lane

WILLIAM   right up to the door

MARY   out of Francis' sight

BOTH   we stand there

(Beat.)

WILLIAM   she seems a bit nervous

MARY   does he want to come in?

WILLIAM   I smile at her, I can't help it

MARY   he laughs

WILLIAM   I smile

MARY   that funny laugh

WILLIAM   I smile

MARY   and I laugh too and I open the door

WILLIAM   she opens the door

MARY   Do you want to come in?

WILLIAM   yes, yes I do very much.

MARY   he says nothing

WILLIAM   yes, yes I do very much.

MARY   he says nothing— Well don't just stand there letting in the cold air.

WILLIAM   I enter her house

MARY   he enters my house!

WILLIAM   I enter her house!

MARY   my parents asleep, I close the door

WILLIAM   she closes the door, pitch black

MARY   I light the lamp

   (Beat.)

WILLIAM   Nice place.

MARY   Thank you. Fire's out, but it's warmer than out there anyway. Do you want to take your boots off?

WILLIAM   yes, yes I do very much.

MARY   William, your boots, do you want to take them off?

WILLIAM   I'd like to, Mary, thanks…but I shouldn't stay for long, I don't want Francis to freeze to death.

MARY   All right.

WILLIAM   And my folks will be worried as well, I
              should be getting home, it must be past four
              o'clock.

MARY   All right, all right, I just thought you might
              like to warm up your feet.

WILLIAM   They're fine. Thank you.

MARY   How long have you to walk?

WILLIAM   Well, we're up past Warren's Mill, so from
              here it's probably a good hour and a bit.

MARY   Oh dear, I'm sorry, you needn't have taken
              me.

WILLIAM   No, it was no trouble, I rather liked it...
              You're some pretty, Mary Tuplin.

MARY   Please, you mustn't compliment me.

WILLIAM   Why not?

MARY   One shouldn't be paid a compliment if one is
              undeserving.

WILLIAM   And you're undeserving...? You're not.
              You're beautiful, Mary. You are.

MARY   Can we talk about something else?

WILLIAM   Like what?

MARY   I don't know, anything.

WILLIAM   Actually I should get going.

MARY   You just got in. You can't be warm yet.

WILLIAM   No, I really should. My mother won't go to
              bed till I'm home.

MARY   Really?

WILLIAM   Yes.

MARY   How awful. My parents usually retire before
              any of us.

WILLIAM   Hm.

MARY   They're very sound sleepers as well…nothing
              can wake them…

WILLIAM   Not my parents… All right, I must be off.

MARY   his hand on my cheek, it's cold but it's nice

WILLIAM   I step closer to her, her breath on my face

MARY   and he leans towards, looking at me

WILLIAM   my eyes open

MARY   looking at me, I can't breathe

WILLIAM   her breath on my face

MARY   I can't breathe

WILLIAM   her breath in the

BOTH   air

MARY   I can't breathe

  (Beat.)

WILLIAM   I leave

MARY   we talk first

  (Beat.)

WILLIAM   then I leave

MARY   we talk, "a sleigh ride on Sunday" he says,
            "I'll come pick you up, this Sunday evening
            I'll come by with a sleigh and we'll go for a
            ride," and I agree and I agree and I agree!

WILLIAM   she seems not to mind that she'll see me
            again!… Sunday evening with a sleigh then, I
            say, Sunday evening…

MARY   Yes.

(Beat.)

WILLIAM   a walk home in the cold, I puff from the pipe

MARY   I creep up the stairs, listen at the door

WILLIAM   teasing from Francis, "short v-v-visit s-s-sent home" those sorts of things

MARY   my parents snoring, I open the door and crawl into bed

WILLIAM   but she wanted me back

MARY   and I lie awake to the sound of my parents asleep in the bed next to mine and I think

WILLIAM   on Sunday I say she wishes to see me again and so there

MARY   is this love?

WILLIAM   and I'm lying awake, I can't get to sleep

MARY   William Millman

WILLIAM   Mary Tuplin

BOTH   I can't get to sleep, is this love?

(Beat.)

WILLIAM   A GENTLEMAN CALLER ON A SUNDAY
            EVENING!

MARY   A GENTLEMAN CALLER ON A SUNDAY
            EVENING!

WILLIAM   without a sleigh

MARY   he never brought a sleigh!

WILLIAM   I came though, I came, late Sunday, the
            family

MARY   he never brought a sleigh

WILLIAM   I'm sorry

MARY   so we sit at home with my family and talk,
            John Junior running around, Jacob still
            peeling potatoes for being a bad chaperone,
            my parents fussing, my older sister Christy
            making eyes, my God

WILLIAM   I'm sorry, I came though, didn't I?

MARY   yes, he came!

BOTH   A GENTLEMAN CALLER ON A SUNDAY
            EVENING!

MARY   Good night, Papa. Well that was exciting.

WILLIAM   It was.

MARY   I'm so sorry, I do apologize. My family is not
                   used to seeing boys around the house.

WILLIAM   No bother.

MARY   Nerve racking.

WILLIAM   Are you cold?

MARY   My father puts the fire out well before he
                   goes to bed. Can't imagine why? Says it
                   saves firewood. Stingy old man. I'm sorry it's
                   so cold.

WILLIAM   I'm fine. Probably does it to force you to
                   retire early, don't you think?

MARY   Well it's not going to work tonight.

WILLIAM   ...I can stay for a while, if that's what you're
                   getting at. My folks think I'm with John
                   Profit tonight.

MARY   John Profit?

WILLIAM   Yes, a friend of mine.

MARY   He is my teacher!

WILLIAM   Oh yes, I guess he would be now, just started teaching.

MARY   Yes, just this year. He's handsome, William, he's a friend of yours?

WILLIAM   we talk about John and my friends and the folks we both know

MARY   How is it possible that we've never met before?

WILLIAM   ...I'm going to not be respectable here and tell you the truth.

MARY   All right.

WILLIAM   I tell her the truth.

MARY   All right.

WILLIAM   I tell her I've seen her, I've seen her before.

MARY   I know.

WILLIAM   No, I've seen her before. I'd stare. Quite a lot.

MARY   Cut it out, you did not.

WILLIAM   I did too, I tell her...and when I saw her walk
            in to the Bryenton's that evening, that
            Tuesday evening, that New Year's Eve, I
            thought: this is my chance, I thought: I must
            speak to her, I may never get to again.

MARY   Do stop it. Did you really?

WILLIAM   Yes! I thought: I may never get this chance
            again, and that's when I gathered enough
            courage to approach her.

MARY   Plus you were quite drunk.

WILLIAM   A little perhaps. Courage, you know— But I
            tell her the truth, a little embarrassing but it is
            the truth.

MARY   My father doesn't approve of drinking.

WILLIAM   Well I'm not courting your father, am I?

MARY   Oh so you're Courting me, are you, well it's
            my mother who wouldn't approve of
            that... They liked you though, I think. Mother
            and Father.

WILLIAM   Your father hardly said a word to me.

MARY   That's a good sign though. And when I told
              Christy about you she immediately spread it
              like wildfire to the rest of my brothers and
              sisters that you were my "boyfriend," so
              that's why they've been looking at you and
              giggling all night. I'm sorry.

WILLIAM   That's fine, I rather enjoyed it. I love John
              Junior! He's so sweet, how old is he?

MARY   Just turned three.

WILLIAM   They're wild at that age, eh?

MARY   Oh, he was tame tonight. You should see him
              when he eats a candy or two, he's
              uncontrollable.

WILLIAM   I love him!

MARY   Yes, definitely the wild one of us all. Well,
              the others were a little giddy tonight too, you
              understand— Why didn't you bring your
              sleigh?! You promised!

WILLIAM   I never promised.

MARY   I know, it's all right, maybe next time.

WILLIAM   Oh, so there will be a next time, will there?

MARY   I never said that. I said maybe. If you're
           good.

WILLIAM   Ah.

MARY   Meaning you've still got a chance to redeem
           yourself tonight.

WILLIAM   ...All right.

   (Beat.)

WILLIAM   So the family seems to not mind me, eh?

MARY   It appears that way, can't imagine why...

WILLIAM   ...I like the way you smile.

MARY   You're always complimenting me, you must
           stop it.

WILLIAM   Why?

MARY   ...I like it

   (Beat.)

WILLIAM   It is getting quite chilly in here actually.

MARY   It might be warmer in the parlor. The fire's
           probably still kind of warm and there's
           blankets if you'd like...

WILLIAM   …Sounds lovely.

(They touch.)

WILLIAM   keep your eyes on the girl

MARY   this look in his eyes

WILLIAM   grab onto her hand

MARY   and my hand reaching out

WILLIAM   letting go, reaching out

MARY   and we sink

WILLIAM   round the front, to her stomach, her neck

MARY   away slowly down

WILLIAM   slip her under

MARY   we're gone

WILLIAM   in my arms, in the air

MARY   and we sink

WILLIAM   round the front, to her stomach, her neck

MARY   away slowly down

WILLIAM   slip her under

MARY   we're gone, and we sink

WILLIAM   round the front, to her stomach, her neck

MARY   and we sink

WILLIAM   round the front, to her stomach

MARY   we're gone, and we sink

WILLIAM   slowly down, to her stomach, we're gone

MARY   and we sink slowly down

WILLIAM   slip her under

MARY   we're gone, for eternity

WILLIAM   gone

MARY   till forever

WILLIAM   till

   (Beat.)

WILLIAM   "Mary?"

MARY   my father calls down in the middle of the
    night

WILLIAM   "Mary, it's past midnight, why aren't you in bed?"

MARY   Oh God, get going!—we scramble and pray he won't come down the stairs

WILLIAM   trip over my trousers— Where are my boots?

MARY   Get them on outside, quickly now, quickly!

WILLIAM   I thought you said nothing could wake them— "Mary!?"

MARY   I *lied* get outside, quickly, outside.

WILLIAM   she lied?

MARY   just a fib— Coming, Pa!

WILLIAM   the rush of cold air, my feet in the snow, hurry round the back to the shadow of a tree and I stop. Breathe.

MARY   listen for movement upstairs...there is none... —Coming! ...so, carefully now fold the blankets...tiptoe upstairs to the bedroom I share with my parents, and explain...

WILLIAM   no noise in the house, must've gone back to
            sleep...throw my coat on the ground, wrestle
            my boots onto my soaking feet, do up my
            shirt, shake my coat off, put it on, and make
            my way home...

MARY   Sorry to frighten you, Papa. We were talking
            downstairs, we lost track of time.

    (Beat.)

WILLIAM   and on Tuesday...that Tuesday I walk down
            Mud Road towards Mary's

MARY   Sorry to frighten you, Papa, we lost track of
            time.

WILLIAM   and I stop at the bridge, that same bridge we
            kicked snow from...at the end of the bridge,
            and look back

MARY   is this love?

WILLIAM   and I carve it on the wood, under the deck, on
            Tuesday...that Tuesday I go out and I carve it
            under the bridge with my knife

MARY   is this love?

WILLIAM   Mary Tuplin

MARY   William Millman

WILLIAM   January 5th, 1887

MARY   on Tuesday

WILLIAM   I carve it

BOTH   that Tuesday

MARY   I tell my sister Christy

WILLIAM   on Tuesday

MARY   I'm in love!

WILLIAM   I lie down and reach up and I carve it—Mary
            Tuplin!

MARY   William Millman!

WILLIAM   January 5th, 1887—and as soon as I carve
            it...I know it is true

MARY   it is true!... It is true, I'm in love!

  (Beat.)

MARY   Francis, where's William? Why hasn't he
            come by?

WILLIAM   next Sunday the Bryenton's take me aside

MARY   I saw him at church and he turned the other
              way.

WILLIAM   they ask how things are with the young
              Tuplin girl— Oh, I visited her, met her
              family and all.

MARY   My family liked him, they wonder where he
              is.

WILLIAM   I cared for her family, though her father quite
              scared me.

MARY   He needn't be scared of my father, he's fine.

WILLIAM   And I quite cared for Mary.

MARY   Does he not care for me?

WILLIAM   Yes, I cared quite a lot...but she did not feel
              the same towards me... "Oh poor boy, that's
              too bad...but more time for your practice"
              Mr. Bryenton chuckles and I chuckle too and
              sit down to the piano and play...

MARY   If he feels like it, Francis, tell him he's
              welcome...tell him he can write.

WILLIAM   not wanting to write, too scared to visit, I go
              to John Profit

MARY   John Profit

WILLIAM   my friend

MARY   my teacher

BOTH   John Profit

WILLIAM   Tell Mary Tuplin I feel it was a mistake.

MARY   whispers "William Millman feels it was a mistake."

WILLIAM   I can't see her anymore.

MARY   "He can't see you anymore."

WILLIAM   I don't like her.

MARY   …"doesn't like you."

(Beat.)

WILLIAM   Francis brags "I've become p-p-pretty good friends with that MMMary Tuplin."

MARY   Christy, what does this mean?

WILLIAM   "She j-j-jokes about you with her ssisters and ffriends, William."

MARY   Oh my God, are you sure, Christy? oh my God.

WILLIAM   "She g-g-giggles about you behind the—church on Sundays, yes I've become *quite close* friends with Mary."

MARY   Oh my God, Christy, please don't tell, please don't tell, are you sure?

WILLIAM   but I try to forget about her

MARY   William? please, William?

WILLIAM   and I try to not think about her

MARY   Francis, where's William?

WILLIAM   and I try to not dream about her

MARY   Mr. Profit, where's William?

WILLIAM   I am trying to forget about her!

MARY   Mr. Bryenton, it is imperative that I speak with William Millman!

WILLIAM   "William, it is *imperative* that Mary Tuplin speak with you."

MARY   but I don't tell the reason

WILLIAM   "She would not tell the reason."

BOTH   Please

WILLIAM   I am trying to forget about her.

MARY   "He is trying to forget about you, Mary. It seems you may have broken his heart. My advice would be to send him a letter, mutter mutter, a letter."

WILLIAM   don't send me a letter

MARY   William, Dear William

WILLIAM   don't send me a letter

MARY   William, Dear William

WILLIAM   I don't even read it. I lean out my window and by the light of the moon, strike a match and the flame...

MARY   Dear William

WILLIAM   I don't even read it

    (Beat.)

WILLIAM   I help out my father on the farm

MARY   tansy, quinine, pennyroyal, rue...ergot of rye, cotton root, savin

WILLIAM   take care of my mother "William, I'm fine, now go learn your theory."

MARY   some field, or swamp, or grove contains the
            needful poison; and forthwith it is swallowed

WILLIAM   and I practice piano

MARY   if medicines fail: bleedings, hot baths, violent
            exercises, consumption of large quantities of
            gin

WILLIAM   save money for college

MARY   if these don't prevail: attempt a dilation of the
            cervix with slippery elm, a sponge tent, or
            catheter

WILLIAM   and time just goes by

MARY   if still not beyond the sixteenth week

WILLIAM   and time just goes by

MARY   "Too much time has gone by," Christy
            says... "It's too late now to try anything
            else."

    (Beat.)

MARY   I'm sorry, Mama, I'm sorry, I'm
            sorry—Papa!

WILLIAM   "Mary Tuplin's dropped from school," says
            John Profit

MARY   I tried to be rid of it, Christy and I, we tried.

WILLIAM   Is she sick? I ask John, he's not sure

MARY   William Millman, you remember…he came
            about New Year's.

WILLIAM   he asks "What happened at New Year's?"

BOTH   and I breathe… We were downstairs in the
            parlor, under some blankets.

WILLIAM   "You're teasing!" he says— No I'm not.

BOTH   We did, it's the truth.

MARY   I'm sorry.

WILLIAM   "Your parents will kill you if they ever find
            out!"

BOTH   I know

MARY   "you'll take care of it, Mary, or you know I
            will"

BOTH   I know

MARY   father

BOTH   I know…

MARY   and a letter to the Bryenton's— Tell William
              to meet me.

BOTH   on Sunday

WILLIAM   Mr. Bryenton takes me aside

MARY   Tell him to meet me down at my gate.

WILLIAM   "You must meet Mary Tuplin down at her
              gate!"

BOTH   Why?

MARY   Tell him why!

WILLIAM   And she's saying it's mine?!

MARY   It's William Millman's for sure.

    (Beat.)

WILLIAM   a gentleman caller on a Sunday evening

MARY   waiting for William

WILLIAM   I walk down Mud Road

MARY   six months since that night

WILLIAM   six months, half a year since I walked down this road, we kicked snow from this bridge, I crept under this bridge with my knife

MARY   six months

WILLIAM   half a year

BOTH   and you find it goes by with the blink of an eye...

WILLIAM   I spoke not one word to Mary in that whole half a year

MARY   not one word...

WILLIAM   a gentleman caller on a Sunday evening

MARY   a gentleman caller on a Sunday evening...

WILLIAM   Thank you for meeting.

MARY   Thank you for coming... How Are you?

WILLIAM   Fine. You?

MARY   I've been better. Keeping busy?

WILLIAM   Yes. On the piano a lot more these days. Three times a week. Hoping to be accepted to college this autumn... You're feeling all right?

MARY   Under the circumstances.

WILLIAM   How's your family?

MARY   Little John is sick, you remember him.

WILLIAM   John Junior? of course I do. Is he bad?

MARY   Yes, very bad.

WILLIAM   Oh no, I'm sorry. Give him my love, and my regards to the family as well.

MARY   How's your family?

WILLIAM   Doing all right... Yes, they're doing all right... You look healthy.

MARY   Do I?

WILLIAM   Yes.

MARY   Thank you. I don't feel it.

    (Beat.)

WILLIAM   and it's questions upon questions upon talk about *blame*

MARY   William—

WILLIAM   No, that's what Mr. Bryenton said is all, that the blame is on me... It's funny. The Bryenton's think it's partly *their* fault: they still believe *they* introduced us.

MARY   and it's answers upon questions upon talk about *truth*

WILLIAM   And you're saying it's mine.

MARY   Yes, that's the truth.

WILLIAM   Truth?

MARY   Yes.

WILLIAM   Not just teasing?

MARY   No.

WILLIAM   You're sure?

MARY   Yes.

WILLIAM   And does anyone know...that you're saying it was me?

MARY   The Bryenton's know, and my family of course.

WILLIAM   You told your family you thought it was me?

MARY   Yes.

WILLIAM   I look up to the house, her father in the
            window

MARY   I turn around, Papa staring at us— And do
            your parents know?

WILLIAM   They can't know, they'd kill me. That's why
            I couldn't see you again.

MARY   Why?

WILLIAM   My folks…

MARY   Yes.

WILLIAM   They want me to go to college. They say a
            social life gets in the way.

MARY   Truth?

WILLIAM   Yes.

MARY   The only reason you couldn't see me again?
            Your folks?

WILLIAM   Yes.

MARY   Truth?

WILLIAM   Yes…not only that. I felt bad.

MARY   Bad?

WILLIAM   It was a sin, Mary.

MARY   …It doesn't have to be.

   (Beat.)

WILLIAM   and her hand on her tummy

MARY   it's six months for sure

WILLIAM   the wind rushes by

MARY   with this look in his eyes

WILLIAM   I thought I was quite careful

MARY   this look in his eyes

WILLIAM   I thought I was quite careful.

MARY   Sorry?

WILLIAM   I said I thought I was quite careful, Mary. I mean, I tried to do just what they all say, to…pull myself out before like…

MARY   Well—

WILLIAM   No, I was quite careful, Mary. I made sure.

MARY   William…you're the only one I've been with that way.

WILLIAM   …I don't know, Mary.

MARY   About what?

WILLIAM   Like I said, I was quite careful.

MARY   William.

WILLIAM   No, Mary—

MARY   William, you realize what you are saying about me.

(Beat.)

WILLIAM   How is Francis?

MARY   Sorry?

WILLIAM   From what I hear you and Francis were pretty sweet on each other.

MARY   What are you talking about?

WILLIAM   He tells me you became quite close friends.

MARY   I haven't seen him for months.

WILLIAM   Why not?

MARY   I don't know, he stopped calling round,
                WHAT did he tell you?

WILLIAM   He told me you had become *quite close*.

MARY   Oh my God.

WILLIAM   I'm only telling you what he said.

MARY   Well, he's LYING, William. This child is
                yours.

WILLIAM   ...All right, Mary, I've got to meet you some
                other time. My folks will be wondering where
                I am.

MARY   William. My father wanted me to make sure
                you knew some things.

WILLIAM   All right, what?

MARY   That this will cost money.

WILLIAM   I know.

MARY   And that he and my mother will not take on
                too much of the responsibility.

WILLIAM   All right.

MARY   And that...my reputation will not suffer
                because of this.

WILLIAM   All right.

MARY   So they wonder how you feel about me. And
            how I feel about you. Us. They wonder if it's
            a possibility. I told them it wasn't really, after
            all, you didn't want to see me again, but—

WILLIAM   No, I did WANT to, Mary... I couldn't.
            Listen, I really have to be off. I'll meet you
            on Tuesday, is that all right? I'm away
            tomorrow, doing my conservatory, but I can
            meet you Tuesday evening, all right?

MARY   Sure.

WILLIAM   Sundown?

MARY   Sure. Meet me here.

WILLIAM   All right. See you then.

MARY   turn back up the lane, Papa still stands there

WILLIAM   head back up Mud Road, quicken my pace

MARY   Papa still stands there— William? What do I
            tell my father?

WILLIAM   We're going to meet on Tuesday and work
            something out.

MARY   we're going to meet on Tuesday and work
              something out

WILLIAM   Hey...I hope John Junior feels better.

MARY   Me too. Thank you.

BOTH   We're going to meet on Tuesday and work
              something out.

   (Beat.)

MARY   and on Tuesday

WILLIAM   at sunset

BOTH   that Tuesday

WILLIAM   I make my way towards Mary's, down Mud
              Road, across that bridge

MARY   wait by the gate, I'm alone at home, caring
              for the Bryenton's little one...seems they feel
              the sudden desire to train me in mothering

WILLIAM   the breeze is nice, fans the sweat from my
              face

MARY   just before sunset

WILLIAM   and there she stands

MARY   by the gate

WILLIAM   with a little one in her arms

MARY   She's the Bryenton's, I'm taking care of her.

WILLIAM   that's what she'll look like, carrying a child

MARY   I can see it in his eyes

WILLIAM   beautiful…and she blushes, she almost
            blushes but

MARY   My family will be home any minute.

WILLIAM   So?

MARY   You don't want to be here, trust me.

WILLIAM   What's wrong?

MARY   Go hide in the bushes and I'll meet you there.

WILLIAM   and the moment she says it, she turns back to
            the house, so I run across the road to the
            trees, duck down

BOTH   and I wait

MARY   at the window for my folks to arrive…
            —Down to the river!

WILLIAM   she whispers

MARY   I do?

WILLIAM   yes, you do

MARY   Down to the river!

WILLIAM   Why? What's the hurry?

MARY   My father just arrived, he wants to talk with you in person, he'll be out any minute.

WILLIAM   and I quicken my pace

MARY   move a branch from my way

WILLIAM   it snaps back in my face

MARY   we duck under leaves, over roots, through the trees

WILLIAM   Why does he want to talk with me?

MARY   He doesn't think we can work something out by ourselves. He wants to get your parents involved.

WILLIAM   Whoa.

MARY   I know and I tried to tell him that we'd work it out, just you and me.

BOTH   take a quick look back

WILLIAM   Does he know where you are?

MARY   I ran out without saying a word. Come, this way.

WILLIAM   ...and we come to the clearing, to the bank of the river

MARY   and we stand by the trees, and the river runs by

WILLIAM   across the river, a field

MARY   across the field, more trees

WILLIAM   and above the trees

BOTH   the sun caresses the skyline...

WILLIAM   So he's pretty serious, eh?

MARY   Well, I think he's got a right to be, William.

WILLIAM   "Mary?"

MARY   my father calls from the road

WILLIAM   "Mary, where are you?"

(Beat.)

            "You come back to the house this instant,
            Mary."

(Beat.)

            "William Millman."

(Beat.)

            "I know you're out there."

MARY   William.

WILLIAM   "I know that you're out there."

MARY   William. Listen to me. He won't come down
            here, and even if he did, we'd hear him
            through the trees. So calm down, sit beside
            me and let's talk or we'll never get back up
            there.

WILLIAM   and she smiles

MARY   and he laughs

WILLIAM   I...smile

MARY   **that funny laugh**

(Beat.)

WILLIAM   Francis.

MARY   Francis? What about him?

WILLIAM   We had a good talk.

MARY   You still believe—?

WILLIAM   No. I don't know what to believe.

MARY   No?

WILLIAM   No, I don't know who or what to believe.

MARY   and it's talk of the letter

WILLIAM   Did you send me a letter?

MARY   A letter?

WILLIAM   Around March, I think?

MARY   Yes.

WILLIAM   It wasn't from Francis?

MARY   No.

WILLIAM   Truth?

MARY   Yes. You thought it was Francis?

WILLIAM   No, I didn't know. I didn't even read it.

MARY   What?

WILLIAM   I didn't even read it. I burned it.

MARY   You didn't even read it?

WILLIAM   No.

MARY   So you never knew?

WILLIAM   What.

MARY   That you were to meet me at the Bryenton's cream social.

WILLIAM   No.

MARY   That I was expecting a child, you never even knew?

WILLIAM   Not till Mr. Bryenton told me on Sunday.

MARY   Truth?

WILLIAM   Yes.

MARY   And why did you burn it?

WILLIAM   I was trying to forget about you, I thought it might bring me some peace.

MARY   Some peace?

WILLIAM   I had a suspicion it was from Francis anyway.

MARY   My letter? From Francis?

WILLIAM   Yes, it could have been Francis taking one of his pokes at me.

MARY   How?

WILLIAM   He'd always rub it in that he was calling on you and that you and he would laugh about me.

MARY   Laugh?

WILLIAM   Yes, he told me you'd poke fun at the time we spent together.

MARY   Poke fun?

WILLIAM   You'd giggle behind the church with your sisters and friends.

MARY   No, William, no. No, not at all. I cared for you. My family cared for you.

(Beat.)

WILLIAM   That man up there actually cared for me?

MARY   Believe it or not...

WILLIAM   I cared for you too, Mary...and the breeze
            through her hair

MARY   my reflection in his eyes

WILLIAM   I have to look away

MARY   needing a touch

WILLIAM   wanting to reach

MARY   trying to stay

WILLIAM   May I?

(She nods. He reaches out. She looks down to her tummy.)

MARY   And here I thought you meant...by not
            meeting me, by not seeing me...I thought you
            meant I should get rid of it.

WILLIAM   No. I didn't even know. I had no idea... Why
            didn't you?

MARY   What do you mean?

WILLIAM   Get rid of it...

MARY   It wasn't for lack of trying...

  (Beat.)

WILLIAM   noise by the road

MARY   up near the road, voices of men, walking
              through trees

WILLIAM   They're coming down here!

MARY   My father with others, he must really be
              angry.

WILLIAM   Oh God, let's go, let's go, Mary, now!

MARY   Where?

WILLIAM   Away, down the river, along the bank to the
              bridge.

MARY   My father will kill me, we should really head
              back.

WILLIAM   What?! and say what?

MARY   We're sorry, we've worked something out,
              he'll understand.

WILLIAM   You mean LIE?

MARY   No, we've worked something out, we care for each other. Come on, he's going to kill me for running away.

WILLIAM   Kill you? he'll kill me!

MARY   Don't worry, William, you tell him what you just told me, he'll be fine, we'll be together.

WILLIAM   ...Mary, follow me.

MARY   Where?

WILLIAM   Away, just follow, we need to talk more.

MARY   What is wrong?

WILLIAM   Your father and his hunting party that's what's wrong!

MARY   No, William. What is wrong?

WILLIAM   I can't do this, I can't!

MARY   What are you talking about?

WILLIAM   I can't be with you, Mary. I can't and I won't.

MARY   ...this look in his eyes, he's telling the truth, not very respectable but he's telling the truth

WILLIAM   I can't, I'm sorry. Look, either follow me
            now and we'll work something out, or we'll
            talk later; I can't be standing here like a dope
            when your father comes crashing out of those
            trees.

MARY   and the snap of a branch, even closer now

WILLIAM   I grab her hand, we run up the river

MARY   holding on tight, he pulls me along, I stumble
            on the rocks and cry out in pain

WILLIAM   but I'm still holding on, we scramble up the
            bank, in the trees, out of sight

MARY   one hand in his, the other on my belly

WILLIAM   we crouch in the trees... —Are you all right?

MARY   I'll be fine.

WILLIAM   Are you sure?

MARY   I'll be fine.

WILLIAM   her pain, her breathing, her eyes on the
            ground

MARY   I feel him staring at me

WILLIAM   Follow me further and we'll work something out.

MARY   he moves the branches away from my face

WILLIAM   and we creep in silence till we get to the bridge

MARY   no one around

WILLIAM   we dash for the bank

MARY   slide under the deck

WILLIAM   and up out of sight

BOTH   …we sit there, still, still holding hands…

MARY   the river below us

WILLIAM   the bridge just above

MARY   and he nods to some carving on the underside of the wood

BOTH   …Mary Tuplin, William Millman—January 5th, 1887…

WILLIAM   I carved it the Tuesday after… I was on my way to call on you, and I stopped here and carved it… —I need to leave home, Mary. I need to leave Margate.

MARY   Why?

WILLIAM   I'm going to college in autumn for my music
            and I'm not coming back.

MARY   I'll come with you.

WILLIAM   You can't.

MARY   Why not?

WILLIAM   My father runs a tight house, Mary, a tight,
            strict house.

MARY   So? So you're leaving.

WILLIAM   That's right, I am. And I have money enough
            for myself and...no others.

MARY   My parents will give me some money if it
            means going with you, I'm sure they will.

WILLIAM   Mary... No.

MARY   Then what do we do?

WILLIAM   I can give you a little money.

MARY   I don't want your money.

WILLIAM   That's all I can offer.

MARY   I'll wait till you're back.

WILLIAM   I'm not coming back.

MARY   Why can't you stay here?

WILLIAM   I've told you already.

MARY   Have you?

WILLIAM   I'm going to college, I need to leave home.

MARY   And why can't I come?... William!

WILLIAM   No!

MARY   Why can't I come?!... I have an unclaimed
            child in my belly, William. That's how my
            mother put it—unclaimed. Do you know what
            that means? It means I couldn't even go to
            the funeral today. I had to stay home. I
            couldn't even go to my own brother's funeral.
            My family is too embarrassed...

WILLIAM   Funeral?

MARY   You never heard?

WILLIAM   I've been away.

MARY   My little brother John died Sunday night.

WILLIAM   Oh my God. And you couldn't go to his
            funeral?

MARY   I haven't been off the farm for a good while
            now. My parents have actually started to
            ignore me around the house.

WILLIAM   Really?

MARY   You don't understand the shame, do you?

WILLIAM   Yes I do, Mary.

MARY   But it's not written on your body.

WILLIAM   ...and the wind whistles lightly across the
            bridge picking up dust

MARY   carrying it along, across the river, the tiniest
            of ripples on the water

BOTH   and the sun sinks into the earth...

WILLIAM   I want to run away with you. I want to just
            take you by the hand and walk up this river
            and never look back.

MARY   Then do it.

    (Beat.)

WILLIAM   footsteps on the road

MARY   pounding the earth, running above us, right
            on the deck

WILLIAM   dirt trickles down from between the boards

MARY   sand in the light of the sun

WILLIAM   voices of men

MARY   two, I think

WILLIAM   one Mr. Bryenton

MARY   the other my father, they mumble together

WILLIAM   low voices and mutters

BOTH   they stop

WILLIAM   …Oh God

BOTH   silence

MARY   Dear God…

WILLIAM   "William!"

MARY   "Mary!"

BOTH   they don't know we're here

MARY   thank God

WILLIAM   they keep on

MARY   cross the bridge

WILLIAM   and keep on... —I think it's fair to say that
            I'm quite worried.

MARY   What are they doing?

WILLIAM   I bet you ten to one, Mr. Bryenton is taking
            him to my house.

MARY   Really?

WILLIAM   Yup.

MARY   I'm sorry.

WILLIAM   Yup. That's not good.

MARY   What should we do?

WILLIAM   I need to stop them. My folks can't know
            about this.

MARY   crawls out from under the deck

WILLIAM   Listen, Mary, go home. I'll go catch up with
            them and say you're back. We're sorry we
            ran away and everything's settled.

MARY   Everything's not settled.

WILLIAM   LIE, Mary, please. He'll understand if you're
           safe at home, it *will* be settled, he'll
           understand. Now go, Mary, go.

MARY   leaps onto the bridge, but I do not move

WILLIAM   run a couple of steps

MARY   I do not move, he looks over his shoulder, he
           stops, I don't move

WILLIAM   Mary, go. Please.

MARY   I don't move

WILLIAM   Please Mary, go!

MARY   I don't move

WILLIAM   Fine, I'll tell him you're here.

MARY   but before he can leave

WILLIAM   she clutches her dress in her hand

MARY   I work my way up the bank

WILLIAM   Careful, Mary, be careful.

MARY   up the bank to the road

WILLIAM   she stands at the end of the bridge

MARY   he stands in the middle…and my hand
          reaching out

WILLIAM   you let go, you reach out

MARY   letting go, reaching out

WILLIAM   I don't move…and step back, I step back,
          going to run

MARY   I'm coming with you.

WILLIAM   under her breath but I heard it

MARY   I'm coming with you.

WILLIAM   No, Mary, you are going home. We'll work it
          out later.

MARY   one hand holding my dress, the other
          defiantly swinging at my side as I walk

WILLIAM   Mary, calm down.

MARY   No, I'm coming with you, we're going to
          your house right now, let me by.

WILLIAM   Mary.

MARY   No, we'll catch up with my father—let me
          go—we'll march right in to your house— Let
          go of me, William!

WILLIAM   Mary, please, calm down, let's be
           reasonable—

MARY   OW!

WILLIAM   Mary, stop it!

MARY   No! Go tell my father the truth, William!

WILLIAM   You don't understand.

MARY   Go tell *your* father the truth!

WILLIAM   You don't understand!

MARY   Then tell ME the truth!

WILLIAM   I can't.

MARY   and I cry out in pain

WILLIAM   I can't

MARY   and he won't let me go

WILLIAM   I can't

MARY   he won't

WILLIAM   I can't

MARY   he will not let go

WILLIAM   I can't

MARY   There's so many things you just can't do,
            why is that?

WILLIAM   I don't know.

MARY   Fear?

WILLIAM   Yes.

MARY   What have you got to be afraid of?...and this
            look in his eyes

WILLIAM   ...she won't let me go

MARY   William?

WILLIAM   ...she won't let me go

MARY   William?

WILLIAM   ...she sees

MARY   my God!

WILLIAM   she runs

MARY   I run, down the bridge, to the road, along the
            bank

WILLIAM   I follow, she's silent

BOTH   I'm screaming inside

MARY   I fly like the wind

WILLIAM   I follow

MARY   I stumble on the rocks, then run on, don't
              look back

WILLIAM   keep your eyes on the girl

MARY   don't look back

WILLIAM   keep your eyes on the girl

MARY   a hand on my shoulder, I scream

WILLIAM   I've got her, round the front, to her stomach,
              her neck

MARY   and we sink

WILLIAM   round the front, to her stomach, her neck, to
              the water, the edge of the river and—

(She screams.)

WILLIAM   I move but I'm not really there, ringing and
              gripping

MARY   I'm screaming inside

WILLIAM   I can see my hands but they're so far away,
           under water, around her and under

MARY   I'm screaming inside

WILLIAM   and it's loud, louder than anything, drowning
           out everything…and that's what you're doing,
           you breathe in the water

MARY   where am I?

WILLIAM   you're there but your body

MARY   I'm gone

WILLIAM   there's nothing

MARY   the water, the weight…the water takes
           everything

    (Beat.)

WILLIAM   and for a few breaths

BOTH   our child

MARY   has a few breaths

WILLIAM   after your heart has stopped

BOTH   our child

WILLIAM   for a few breaths

MARY   lives beyond its mother

(Beat.)

WILLIAM   and I stand with her, I stand and I walk

MARY   with Mary with child in the blanket of your arms

WILLIAM   I walk

MARY   till forever

WILLIAM   for just a few steps

MARY   till forever

WILLIAM   out into the water, and slip her under…your eyes

MARY   they're open, eyes open

WILLIAM   your eyes

MARY   they're open, eyes open, looking up at you, wondering what you've done, being dragged slowly down…back on land you wander a bit

WILLIAM   under the bridge

MARY   they'll find me, they will know, you will be
              blamed

WILLIAM   should I have buried her?

BOTH   and it's not questions about life and death and
              love, it's not questions like that

MARY   that run through your mind, it's questions like

WILLIAM   should I have buried her? she wouldn't be
              found if I'd buried her

*(The lights fade slowly, till all that remains is a sky of
glowing lanterns.)*

DIRECTOR'S NOTES

DIRECTOR'S NOTES

DIRECTOR'S NOTES

DIRECTOR'S NOTES